I WISH YOU AND YOUR ⋯⋯ VERY
BEST. GOD BLESS!

Earthquakes and Attitudes

Turn Your Obstacles into Opportunities

Earthquakes and Attitudes

Turn Your Obstacles Into Opportunities

by

Gary J. Moore

Foreword by Ken Jones, Ph.D.

Carpe Diem! Publishers
P.O. Box 1994
Loveland, CO 80539

Although the author and publisher have made every effort to ensure the accuracy and completeness of information contained in this book, we assume no responsibility for errors, inaccuracies, omissions, or any inconsistency herein. Any slights of people, places, or organizations are uninten-tional.

First printing 1995

ISBN 0-9646156-0-6

LCCN 95-68934

Editing, design, typesetting, and printing services provided by About Books, Inc., 425 Cedar Street, Buena Vista, CO 81211, (800) 548-1876.

ATTENTION CHURCHES, PROFESSIONAL ORGA-NIZATIONS, CORPORATIONS, UNIVERSITIES, AND COLLEGES: Quantity discounts are available on bulk purchases of this book for educational purposes or fund raising. Special books or book excerpts can also be created to fit specific needs. For information, please contact Carpe Diem! Publishers, P.O. Box 1994, Loveland, CO 80539 or call (970) 667-1610.

Dedication

This book is affectionately dedicated to my wife Rhonda and our three children—Mandy, Jennifer and Josh. All of them went through the "earthquake" with me and it is by virtue of their wonderful attitudes that I've been able to Catch My Second Wind!

Acknowledgment

I would like to express special gratitude to my editor, Phyliss Burdge, who encouraged me to write this book and more. Although she struggles with the devastating effects of M.S., she is a constant inspiration and "a breath of fresh air" to my work.

Table of Contents

Foreword   Dr. Ken Jones 1

Chapter 1   Purely Personal 7

Chapter 2   When the Bottom Drops Out 11

Chapter 3   The Power of Affirmation 15

Chapter 4   Earthquakes and Attitudes 21

Chapter 5   Attitude Is Everything 27

Chapter 6   Disabilities Need Not
                   Disqualify 33

Chapter 7   Attitude Determines Success—
                   Part 1 41

Chapter 8   Attitude Determines Success—
                   Part 2 45

Chapter 9   Attitude Determines Success—
                   Part 3 51

Chapter 10   Got Any Jumper Cables? 59

Conclusion   Aftershock! 65

Foreword

"Catch Your Second Wind"

I first met Gary Moore in December of 1986. The congregation where he preached in Hooker, Oklahoma, had invited me to come and speak for a few days. December was a poor time for a gospel meeting. The weather turned bad. Snow began to fall. In spite of the weather, the congregation still gathered every morning for a seven o'clock assembly and for an evening assembly. After the morning assemblies, Gary and I would bundle up and go out jogging together. We were about the same age and our professional backgrounds were similar. We became instant friends. Gary and Rhonda helped make my time in Hooker a joyful experience.

Approximately one month later, I heard of the accident. I was devastated. Tears filled my eyes each time I thought of what Gary was going through. There was no way to imagine it or really understand it. I couldn't help but think, *What if I had been the one? What would I do?*

I observed Gary's improvement during the next months and years. What I saw was a remarkable story of courage and success. The Gary Moore story is one that should be told all over this nation. I've done my best to tell it as I know it. However, Gary is the one who tells it best. This book is Gary's story. It is a story of sadness, distress, survival, encouragement and victory. No one can read it without being affected for the good.

For some time, I have been saying that life is composed of three kinds of days—highs, lows and ordinaries. The highs are those days when unexpected good news comes. These are days when you can't help but have a smile on your face and laughter in your heart. They don't come often, only once in a great while. The lows are just the opposite. They are the days when unexpected bad news comes or when tragedy strikes. On these days, no smile appears and tears are unceasing. Thankfully, these are also very infrequent. The ordinary days are the common ones. They are the days like most of the other days of life. On these days, we do about the same thing we always do.

On those few days of life we call the highs, my goal has been to celebrate. These days don't come often, so while they are here, capture the moment with celebration. My goal for the ordinary days of life is to make them the best they can be. Ordinary days of life should not fall into the routine of mediocrity.

Each of you can see that it is easy and natural to celebrate the highs. It is more difficult to make more of our ordinary days. Both of these are easier than what is required for the lows. On those days that are lows, the goal must be survival. The best we can hope for on those days that are filled with bad news and tragedy is to survive until they pass. In this book, Gary Moore puts each of us on the road to survival.

Gary Moore is a survivor. He knew tragedy and bad news as a young boy. Losing parents and making a new home with relatives is a shattering experience for anyone. Gary Moore survived. Then the accident came. It started out as an ordinary day, one that quickly became filled with bad news and tragedy. In a flash, the legs he jogged upon, the ones that supported him as he spoke week by week to a loving congregation, the same ones that carried him as he followed his children from place to place, no longer functioned. The use of those legs was suddenly gone—forever. How does a young man lead his family from a wheelchair? How does a preacher preach from a wheelchair? How do you spend the next forty years or so in a wheelchair? These questions and more raced through Gary's mind.

Gary's answer to those questions came as a result of *catching a second wind*. The *second wind* was a renewal of attitude. It was a spirit of determination fostered by right thinking and a refusal to give up. It was a spirit of survival gathered through prayer and encouragement. Most of all, this *second wind* is something Gary says each of us can experience and claim for our own.

Life is filled with problems for each of us. While we each proclaim that life is good, we also realize it is difficult. To survive the hard experiences of life, we must, at times, *catch our second wind*.

This book warms the heart. It encourages each of us. Most of all, it gives a formula for survival. My admiration continues for Gary Moore, his family and all who aided in giving him his *second wind*. The lessons he teaches can literally change any of our lives.

Chapter 1
Purely Personal

"Leave the comfort zone and face life's challenges."
—Mary Lou Retton. First U.S. female gymnast to win an Olympic gold medal (1984 Summer Games)

There are so many things in the course of a lifetime that can't be appraised with a dollar value: finding awe in the presence of a four-year-old literally bursting from anticipation on Christmas morning; experiencing the undying loyalty of a friend throughout life's peaks and valleys; or being blessed with awareness for the joys of life and courage for the trials. The list is inexhaustible. It runs the gamut from a loving relationship between a husband and wife to the seemingly simple accomplishment of raising a hand in greeting to a friend.

Priceless, and perhaps most important as we slug it out every day, is the ability to *catch our second wind*. Without that ability, life is at best a mere existence. Most of us refer to our second wind as *hope*. Hope is our lifeblood. It is the anticipation that circumstances are going to get better. The four-year-old's enthusiasm on Christmas morning illustrates one kind of anticipation. More often, our hope is not built on joyful expectation but on a desire that unpleasant or even devastating conditions will somehow get better—things will work out, a solution lies just around the corner.

> What morale is to an army—
> what momentum is to a football team—
> what rain is to a parched field—
> HOPE is to victorious living!

Pick up any newspaper and you will read of people who never caught their *second wind*:

- The confused husband/father who holds a handgun to his head and weeps, not because he's about to die but, because he's troubled as to why he ever lived.

- The athlete who thinks his *second wind* will never come, so he injects his body with anabolic steroids that will eventually destroy his career and his life.

- The couple who stand in divorce court having found not their earthly heaven in marriage, but instead, their living hell.

People tempted to take drastic, even catastrophic, action need to catch their *second wind* to find hope.

"How trite. That's easy for Gary Moore to say," might be what you're thinking. Maybe I should rephrase the statement. People need to make one final, gut-wrenching effort to dig deep within, turn themselves inside out, have someone shake them by the heels until the only wind they have left is that *second wind*!

My conviction arises from the experiences of my life.

When I was five-years-old, my parents, two older brothers and I lived in Amarillo, Texas. I don't remember much of my life at that age, but I remember that it seemed normal to me. I do, however, have one vivid memory of my dad sitting with us around the kitchen table trying his best to gently explain that our mother had just died. (Years later, I learn she died of complications from diabetes.) I sat in the chapel during her funeral service not understanding "death" or its full impact. I knew she was gone and I knew it was a sad thing because I saw the tears flow from my dad's eyes and heard the sobs of my two older brothers.

The need for a *second wind* didn't mean much to me then. The concept was as obscure as that of death. At five-years-old, I was very resilient and very ignorant about the impact of a mother's death—my mother's death. I still had my dad and my brothers.

Four years later we sat in the same chapel. This time I sobbed along with my brothers. But there were no tears on my dad's cheeks. Our dad had died of complications from stomach surgery. I was ten by then and knew full well the impact of death. What I couldn't understand was *why* I was devastated, for lack of a stronger word, and filled with questions that needed immediate answers. *What would we do? Where would we live? Would my brothers and I stay together, or would we be separated?* I desperately needed a *second wind*, but again the concept eluded me. For the first time in my life, I was truly scared.

God provided the needed grace through an uncle and aunt who lived in the small town of Dalhart, Texas. They took in three rowdy boys without hesitation. They called us their sons. I didn't always understand my Uncle George, but he taught me the value of hard work, integrity, and the value of a good education. My Aunt Gene showed us, and continues to show us, the power of perseverance, the secret of greatness, servitude, and the value of loving relationships.

I became acquainted with the true concept of *hope*. It was here I caught my first *second wind*. I was fortunate to be accepted by my peers, to excel in athletics and even to have a girlfriend or two. After high school graduation, I headed for college. I didn't set any records there, but didn't graduate "magna cum lousy."

Just before I turned twenty-one, my Uncle George died of lung disease. I stood by his hospital bed watching him fight for his life. I realized then just how much I loved and respected him. When he lost the battle, I saw the importance—possibly for the first time—of expressing feelings to a loved one while they are alive.

The musical group, Mike and the Mechanics, expressed it well in a song: "I just wish I had said more in those living years . . ." When you don't, you feel somewhat like the floral arrangements surrounding the casket—nice, but a little late.

Chapter 2

When the Bottom Drops Out

"The greatest discovery of my generation is that human beings can change their lives by changing their attitudes."

—William James

The death of a loved one, especially the "leader figure" at a crucial time in your life, knocks the wind right out of your sails. I was beginning to wonder if I had put some kind of hex on the important people in my life. This was a faulty perception, to be sure, but my perception ran a close race with reality. It even took the lead on occasion. No doubt, I needed a *second wind.*

Once again the Lord provided. Her name was Rhonda Love—a gorgeous, five-foot dynamo of excitement and enthusiasm. At times I thought she must have been injected with a phonograph needle, which was fine with me since I was laid back at that stage of my life. We complemented each other. When I'd dated prior to meeting Rhonda, the girls must have thought I was nearly comatose. I was no Mr. Excitement, that's for sure. On our first date, Rhonda slapped me five times . . . not because I was too fresh but, according to her, she thought I'd died.

The first time I saw Rhonda I knew beyond a shadow of a doubt I was in love and this was the woman I would marry. I remember the exact time and place we first kissed. I experienced a "hormone explosion." Talk about a *second wind!* I was in love and will stay in love all my life. We've been together twenty-three years now and are headed for eternity. I once heard a wise preacher say, "The key to a long and happy marriage is falling in love with the same person each and every day."

Life was so good! The Lord blessed us with three children, each two years apart. For years I had a rewarding career in accounting working with Dale Young, the finest man I've ever known. Then I made a major transition in my life. It began with two years of seminary studies followed by seven years of ministry. The first two years were spent in Van Horn, Texas, a small west-Texas town 110 miles east of El Paso. At times, I felt like Moses in the wilderness. The congregation was small but very close and loving and I was the benefactor. The next five years were served in Hooker, Oklahoma. The congregation of 200 was so good to us, and so active in the church, there were times when I felt guilty accepting my salary. Only Heaven seemed better than the life we led there. At the age of thirty-five, I couldn't remember the last bad day I'd experienced. But the euphoria of the good life can change drastically in a New York minute.

I was driving the school bus route on the morning of January 5, 1987. At 8:00 a.m., three miles southeast of Hooker, I'd just picked up my sixteenth student and was heading back toward town. That was the last thing I remembered for three days. The next scene I recalled was waking up in a hospital room. A nurse was taking my blood pressure and Rhonda was holding my hand. My back felt like there was a hot knife wedged in the middle of it. My head throbbed as though Evandor Holifield had visited vengeance upon it.

Rhonda began the most difficult task of her life. She kissed me softly on the cheek, squeezed my hand firmly and began to relate what had caused the bottom to drop out of our lives. I closed the bus door after picking up my sixteenth student and headed toward town. Fifteen seconds later, I collided with a pickup truck in the next intersection. Upon impact I was ejected and pitched through the windshield to land in a field some thirty feet away from the bus. I got a concussion from hitting the windshield and was knocked colder than a cheap pizza. I hit the ground on my back, exploding four vertebrae and shattering my spinal cord at the waist. I was instantly paralyzed.

The young woman driving the pickup sustained a broken pelvis and her five-year-old son suffered bumps, bruises and trauma. I thank God for their recoveries and for the fact that, miraculously, none of the sixteen children in the bus were seriously injured. It was a freakish accident. I should have seen the pickup and she should have seen the bus. Unfortunately, on that crisp, sunny January morning, neither of us saw the other.

Then Rhonda had to relate the most distressing scenario of all. With broken voice she said, "You are scheduled for back surgery day after tomorrow . . . It doesn't look good . . . The neurologists are almost 100 percent certain you'll never walk again."

The MRI (magnetic resonance imaging) pictures didn't even show a spinal cord at the fracture level. The cord had literally been blown apart at the fracture sight.

I spent two weeks in Wichita, Kansas and then I was flown to Craig Hospital in Denver to begin the long process of rehabilitation. This process consisted of returning to square one in many areas of life. I had to learn to live with a spinal cord injury. A chapter in my life had closed. I was faced with a whole new book. Many nights I lay on that hospital bed engulfed in the dark silence and wondered, *How will my family be affected by all this? What about the astronomical expense? How will I provide? Have I been permanently sidelined as a preacher? How can I possibly fulfill all my duties?*

Question after question . . . until the dark silence began to carry over into the daylight hours. Doubt after doubt . . . to the point that I faced a question I never in my life thought I'd ask myself, *Do I really want to go on living?*

Without a doubt, I needed a *second wind.*

Chapter 3

The Power
of Affirmation

*"Gary was our preacher before (the accident), and we
wouldn't think of it being any other way now."*
—Denton Wiggains, Amarillo Globe News,
Amarillo, Texas

There are times in most people's lives when
quitting looks like the only rational course of action,
when evacuation seems logical and even essential for
survival. During the darkest days of Great Britain's
war with Nazi Germany, England was relentlessly
pounded by German bombers. Night after night
British citizens sought safety from the bombs. Day
after day they saw more of London destroyed. Parlia-
ment called for negotiations with Hitler whose terms
would, of course, be the surrender of Great Britain.
While it seemed everyone called for negotiations and
a ceasing of the bombing, one unlikely-looking, cigar-
smoking British leader refused any dialogue with
Germany. This single individual refused to give in to

Hitler's demands. To him, quitting did not seem the only rational course of action. Quitting didn't seem to *be* an option.

By the very power of the pen, Winston Churchill refused to allow England to quit. He stated that in no way would he deal with a "madman." With six words, repeated time and again, he rallied the people of England. With bulldog tenacity he barked, "Evacuation has never won any war!"

Unfortunately in today's world, evacuation is often expected and even encouraged:

- When romance seems only a memory and marriage begins to take extraordinary effort—vacate the marriage.

- When the job grows tedious and the boss seems unreasonable—vacate the job.

- When school seems to grind on indefinitely and studies begin to overwhelm—vacate the studies.

However, unless you find yourself in a burning building or a sinking ship, evacuation is rarely the best choice. Churchill reminded the Allies that evacuation does not win wars. It is also not the solution to difficult situations such as marital disharmony or job dissatisfaction. Evacuation from education or athletics solves nothing and tends to set a precedent of quitting when the going gets tough. We've all heard the saying, "Winners never quit, and quitters never win." Vacating a situation—quitting—will *never* lead to success or victory. But, I'll be the first to admit that there are certainly times when quitting seems attractive.

I was no Winston Churchill during those first weeks of rehabilitation. I was steeped in battle, you might say, but I had no rallying cry. Part of the time I wasn't sure how to fight and the other part of the time I didn't care about fighting, or winning. I was racked with continual pain. I experienced permanent loss of bladder and bowel functions and I was plagued with a bombardment of questions I wasn't able to answer. The concept of paralysis, *my* paralysis, sat before me like a huge boulder blocking my path . . . to life. On top of everything, I struggled with the plain truth that I was not practicing the principles I'd been preaching for several years. I was ready to quit, to give up the battle. Whether I knew it or not, I was desperately in need of a *second wind*.

Once again God provided. Two-hundred loving people—my congregation in Hooker, Oklahoma—refused to let me quit. Literally hundreds of cards and letters flooded in *every week*. Each word affirmed I would preach and minister again. I was *assured* my experiences would serve to make me more effective. The power of affirmation is incredible! The power of affirmation provides not only the energy but the *will* to fight your way out when your back is against the wall. I received one card that I believe moved me the most. It was a homemade card. A little six-year-old girl had drawn her perception of her preacher sitting in a wheelchair holding a Bible in his hands. Under her crude sketch she wrote, very simply, "I love you, Gary!" As I cried, I firmly resolved *never* to give up.

The affirmations from my congregation did not stop with the words they wrote and sent to me in Denver. One month after the accident, they began work on a new house that would be totally wheelchair accessible. Talk about a *second wind*! They also provided a van equipped with a wheelchair lift and hand-control adaptations so that I could be independent and go about the business of ministering to my congregation.

After six months of intense rehabilitative work, I was ready to resume preaching. The house was completed, and I told the elders of the church there was no way I could pay for a home like that. They handed Rhonda and me the keys and said, "You don't have to; it's our gift to you. It's yours. Whether you stay with us one year or ten years, it will always be yours." The best sermon on love was delivered to me that day. I will forever be indebted to the Church of Christ in Hooker, Oklahoma. Not only for the material gifts they so freely gave, but for their spiritual gift when *they refused to let me quit!* They provided gust after gust of hope.

I continued to serve as preacher of the church in Hooker. For another six years my family and I basked in the warmth of our congregation's love and support. But eventually the number of outside speaking invitations grew and counseling others became a big part of my schedule. I saw the need for a change in direction and a career change that would necessitate a move. So in July of 1993, we packed our bags, said tearful goodbyes and moved to Loveland, Colorado. With access to a large population and major universities, I could continue speaking and counseling while furthering my training in marriage and family therapy.

I agree with George Matthew Adams who said, "There is no such thing as a 'self-made man.' We are made up of thousands of others. Everyone who has ever done a kind deed for us or spoken one word of encouragement to us has entered into the makeup of our character and of our thoughts, as well as our success."

I have always been blessed with the association of good people. To them, I owe all I have achieved in life.

Chapter 4

Earthquakes and Attitudes

"My grandmother was my primary mentor. She was widowed at forty-nine and lived alone for nearly forty years. She never fussed, fretted or complained. She taught me to 'think and thank.' Think of all the things you have to be grateful for, and thank God for all your talents and treasures."

—Dr. Denis Waitley

On the morning of January 17, 1994, the morning I started writing this book, Los Angeles was struck by a major earthquake. At 4:30 a.m. Mother Nature took her finger nail, wedged it beneath the earth's surface and rocked most of southern California. The quake measured 6.6 on the Richter scale and lasted approximately thirty seconds. The damage proved to be enormous:

- The death toll rose to over sixty, with thousands more hurting and homeless.

- Governor Pete Wilson said the damage toll could match hurricane Andrew's $30 billion—the costliest natural disaster in U.S. history.

- Some forty thousand San Fernando Valley residents were without water; thirty-five thousand customers were without natural gas; fifty-two thousand businesses were without electricity.

- Several aftershocks followed the quake and not only caused considerable damage themselves but also heightened the fear of already distraught residents.

The list above is like a child's drawing of the real damage. Lives have been forever changed. That's the nature of earthquakes and of a multitude of disasters. Earthquakes are but one proof we have—as if we'd need more than one—that the Creator of this big ball of dirt could take us out at anytime if He were so inclined.

Earthquakes of the southern California variety are not the only source of upheavals in this life. Disasters wear many faces:

- A terminal disease

- A disabling or fatal accident

- A job layoff

- A bankruptcy

- A divorce

"Disaster: a sudden calamitous event bringing great damage, loss or destruction; a sudden or great misfortune." Webster's definition gives an idea of the magnitude of such an occurrence. But it can't convey the meaning in terms of human suffering, the individual grief, and painful aftermath of disasters.

- A terminal disease in which a body wastes away, usually with great pain, and the face of death clouds every single day;

- A disabling or fatal accident that damages whole families both emotionally and physically, often irreparably;

- A job layoff that sends an honest, hardworking individual into a depression from which he or she may or may not recover;

- A bankruptcy that forces major changes in lifestyle, straining a marriage and relations with family members;

- A divorce, in which much more than the household goods are torn apart.

Attitude is an important key to surviving and rebuilding one's life following a disaster. I see attitude as the perception that I *choose* to adopt within the circumstances of life—good and bad. W. Mitchell often states in his inspirational speeches and in his recent book *The Man Who Would Not Be Defeated*, "It's not what happens to you that matters; it's what you choose to do about it."

Stating it another way, "It's not what happens to you that determines success or failure. It's what happens within you."

Dr. Victor Frankl, a bold, courageous Jew who became a prisoner during the Holocaust, endured years of indignity and humiliation at the hands of the Nazis before he was finally liberated. At the beginning of his ordeal, he was marched into a Gestapo courtroom. His captors had taken away his home and his family, his cherished freedom, his possessions, even his watch and his wedding ring. Then they shaved his head and stripped him. He stood before the German high command, naked and powerless, falsely accused, intimidated and interrogated under glaring lights. He was destitute—a helpless pawn in the hands of brutal and sadistic men driven not by anything logical or reasonable, but by prejudice. Yet Frankl had something they could not strip from him.

Dr. Frankl realized, in time, he still had the power to choose his own attitude. No matter what anyone did to him, regardless of what the future held for him, the choice of attitude was his, and his alone. Bitterness *or* forgiveness, give up *or* go on, hate *or* hope, determination to endure *or* paralysis of self pity—it boiled down to one choice for Victor Frankl.

Earthquakes, or upheavals, are not uncommon. You may never experience anything as unjust as the Holocaust, or as frightening as the earthquakes in southern California, or as life changing as my spinal cord injury. But if I'm certain of anything at all, I'm certain of this. You have your own earthquake story to tell. Where you are now, in terms of recovery, has been determined not so much by the event that shook everything familiar out of its place, but by your attitude toward the event.

The contractor who installed your bathroom may have gotten marble from the same quarry used by Michelangelo. The marble held different visions for the artisan and the artist, hence the difference between a work of art and a new bathroom. Now, it's quite possible Michelangelo could have made a living as a contractor, but he chose to go for more.

We *cannot* be Michelangelo. We *cannot* be anyone other than who we are. But we *can* adopt an attitude about who we are. And we can optimize the raw material we've been given to work with in this life. A beautiful sculpture or a beautiful bathroom are both worthy accomplishments. Leaving the stone in the quarry is not. Attitude will get things moving even when you're not certain at first which way you want things to move.

Whether or not you *catch your second wind* will be determined by your choice of attitude.

Chapter 5

Attitude Is Everything

"When circumstances are such that they won't budge, the only thing that will is your attitude."
—Arthur Gordon, *A Touch of Wonder*

Back in the 1970s, during the rash of airplane hijackings in this country, a plane was hijacked after it left Miami on its way to New York. "Turn this plane around and go to Havana or someone is going to get hurt," ordered the hijacker. The pilot could tell the man was desperate, so he did exactly as he was told. When the hijacker tried to intimidate the passengers, however, he was met with quite a different response. No matter what the gunman did, the passengers laughed. In fact, they roared with laughter.

They laughed all the way to Havana. They laughed while the plane was on the ground and while tense negotiations were going on between Cuban and American authorities. They laughed when the plane was allowed to resume its flight to New York. They turned the whole serious experience into a lark! No one on board was drunk, mind you. In fact, no drinks had been served on the flight.

Strange?

Only one man, besides the pilot and the hijacker, did not laugh. He didn't get the joke. He worried the hijacker would react violently to the laughter of the other passengers. The whole experience was a nightmare for this one passenger—Alan Funt of "Candid Camera" fame.

The presence of Alan Funt aboard the hijacked plane led the other passengers to the erroneous conclusion it was all a prank. At any moment they expected someone to say, "Smile! You're on Candid Camera!" Of course, no one said that. It wasn't a prank. But *thinking* that it was caused the passengers to relax. Their attitude pulled them through a life-threatening situation. (Note: If the opportunity ever presents itself, it is NOT recommended that you laugh at a hijacker or anyone else holding a gun!)

Every once in a while I hear someone say something like, "The worst thing that could possibly happen to me just happened." What happened? Did a friend or a loved one die? Did the doctor discover inoperable cancer? What is the worst thing that could happen to you? I've heard people say, "If that happened to me, I would just die!" It's just an expression . . . or is it? Sometimes we believe it. We believe *we could not survive certain misfortunes* should they occur in our lives.

But guess what, we don't die! It may be the shock that takes longer to wear off but, once it does, we step back from whatever horrible thing has happened and begin to put things into perspective once again.

Some people are defeated in life by an attitude problem. They are finished before they ever start. They give up and snatch defeat from the jaws of victory just because of their mind-set. A victorious attitude would benefit them. Make no mistake about it—developing and maintaining the right attitude and mind-set is grueling work. It takes a large drum of elbow grease and a formidable amount of faith, coupled with a bundle of determination.

Words cannot adequately convey the incredible impact our attitude has on our life. As I sit in a wheelchair and deal with all the ups and downs of spinal cord injury—as well as raising a family, paying the bills, managing a demanding career, and more—I'm convinced, along with Charles Swindoll, that life is 10 percent *what happens* to us and 90 percent *how we respond* to what happens.

How else can anyone explain the unbelievable feats performed by athletes under the most adverse conditions of mental and physical pain? Consider Joe Namath, the quarterback who brought the American Football League (AFL) to parity with the National Football League (NFL) when the New York Jets beat the heavily favored Baltimore Colts in Super Bowl III. The ultimate result was the merger of the two leagues and the birth of the American Football Conference (AFC) and the National Football Conference (NFC) to form the current NFL. At age thirty, he was a quarterback with sixty-five-year-old legs. Although he now has difficulty making one flight of stairs, it was *attitude* that kept this man in the game.

Look at Merlin Olson and his knees. In an interview with a sports reporter, the former Los Angeles Ram All-Pro and Hall-of-Fame defensive lineman admitted, "The year after surgery on my knee, I had to have the fluid drained weekly. Finally, the membrane got so thick they almost had to drive the needle in it with a hammer. I got to the point where I just said, ' . . . get the needle in there and get that stuff out!'"

Joe Namath and Merlin Olson were football giants I grew up watching on Sunday afternoons. The list continues in 1994: Joe Montana suffered a substantial injury in the play-off game with the Los Angeles Raiders but returned to lead Kansas City in a comeback that resulted in victory; Emmett Smith of the Dallas Cowboys played the final four games of the season with a partially separated shoulder but gained over 130 yards rushing in Super Bowl XXVIII to beat the Buffalo Bills and was named the game's Most Valuable Player (MVP). He was also named the MVP of the NFL and once again won the rushing title, even though he missed the first two games of the season. Joe Namath . . . Merlin Olson . . . Joe Montana . . . Emmett Smith . . . *elbow grease* and *attitude*.

Charles Swindoll echoes the undeniable truth that attitude is everything:

> "I believe the single most important decision I make on a day-to-day basis is my choice of attitude. It is more important than my past, my education, my bankroll, my successes or failures, fame or pain, what other people think of me or say about me, my circumstances or my position. It is more important than appearance, giftedness or skill. It will make or break a company . . . a church . . . a home. The remarkable thing is that we have a choice every day

regarding the attitude we will embrace for that day. We cannot change our past . . . we cannot change the fact that people will act in a certain way. We cannot change the inevitable. The only thing we can do is play on the one string we have, and that is our attitude . . . I am convinced that life is 10 percent what happens to us and 90 percent how we react to it."

In the Bible, when Paul and Silas were thrown into jail for preaching Christianity, they sang hymns and gave thanks. Paul encourages us to "Give thanks in all circumstances, for this is God's will for you in Christ Jesus." (I Thessalonians 5:18)

The only real prison in life is the mind. Attitude can either keep you imprisoned, or it can set you free. It is that single ingredient in life that can keep us going or cripple our progress. It alone fuels my fire or assaults my hope. When my attitude is right, there's no barrier too high, no valley too deep, no dream too extreme, no challenge too great.

The earthquake in southern California changed the lives of thousands, possibly even millions of people. For many, life will never be the same. The ultimate determining factor will not be the earthquake itself, but the choice of attitude and a whole lot of elbow grease.

Chapter 6

Disabilities Need Not Disqualify

"When people are discharged from their jobs in industry, it's been my finding that social incompetence (a poor attitude) accounts for 60 to 80 percent of the failures. Only 20 to 40 percent are due to technical incompetence."

—Dr. William Menniger

The damage caused by the California earthquake on January 17, 1994, should never be underestimated. It was truly a nightmare in the reality of life. When the dust cleared:

- People had lost their lives. Sixteen died in the three-story Northridge Meadows apartment building that was flattened to two stories within seconds. Seven died in homes that collapsed. Several suffered heart attacks as a direct result of the quake. Some were crushed to death as they attempted to locate loved ones. The oldest victim was ninety-two; the youngest was four.

- Marc Yobs, 32, and Karen Osterhoet, 30, lived the quintessential southern California life. They were planning marriage. Then their million-dollar dream home was lifted right off its foundation, and it was tossed down a hillside. They had no insurance to cover earthquake damage.

- Gennady Khaytman, 45, spent most waking moments studying, in hopes of becoming an American doctor. Three years ago, he moved from Kiev, in the Ukraine, to California. During the quake, Khaytman was knocked down the steps outside his apartment. His head hit the pavement hard, and he suffered an irreversible head injury. Head injuries, like spinal cord injuries, are very unforgiving. His dream turned to a nightmare in a matter of seconds.

- Elizabeth Brace, 37, was the only casualty in San Bernadino County, one hundred miles from the epicenter. Her first thought was to check on her five-year-old daughter and sixteen-month-old son who were both asleep in their rooms across the hallway. Her husband Tom heard a bang, ran after her and found her unconscious. She died in the hospital an hour later. The emergency room doctor found no apparent cause, but he said, "If it's possible, she died of fright."

It's obvious in these four examples that lives have been changed drastically. For those who died, loved ones live on. Some will pull through with the help of family, friends, and possibly therapy. Others will be destroyed by their circumstances. The final outcome will be determined by *attitude*. Circumstances are often out of our control, but attitude is not. Thank God, we have control over the attitudes we choose to have.

Upheavals of this proportion do happen occasionally in our lives. No matter what form disasters take, our foundations shake and all that has been familiar topples around us. We stand in a mental or physical wasteland and search for an outstretched hand. There is a God in Heaven Who is more powerful than any earthquake, any disaster whose path we may cross. In I Corinthians 10:13, He gives us His written guarantee He will not allow more to be put upon us than we're able to bear with His resources.

It is certain that some upheavals in life are more catastrophic than others. It's also true the smaller ones can make us or break us. If we're honest, we must admit that we spend more of our time concentrating on, or stressed out over, the things outside our control than we do giving attention and energy to what remains within our scope of power . . . our choice of attitude. Stop and think about a few of the things that suck up our attention and energy, all of them inescapable (and some demoralizing):

- The weather, the temperature, the wind;

- People's actions and reactions—especially the criticisms;

- Who won or lost the ball game (especially when your son or daughter is involved);

- Delays at airports, waiting in lines, rush-hour traffic;

- Results of an x-ray;

- The cost of groceries, gasoline, clothes, cars—everything;

- On-the-job irritations, disappointments, work load.

The greatest waste of energy in our ecologically-minded world of the 1990s does not involve electricity or natural gas or any other product—it's the energy we waste fighting the inevitables. We suffer from this futile fight. We grow sour. We get ulcers. We become twisted, negative, tightfisted combatants. Some of us actually die from stress-related illnesses attributed to fighting the inevitables.

Dozens of comprehensive studies have established this fact. One famous study called "Broken Heart" researched the mortality rate of 4,500 widowers within six months of their wives' deaths. Compared with other men the same age, the widowers had a mortality rate 40 percent higher.

Without a doubt, the death of a spouse is a huge upheaval. According to the University of Washington School of Medicine Stress Scale, the death of a mate is the highest stress-producing ordeal anyone can experience. It is a handicap in great proportion, more paralysing than a spinal cord injury. It is, indeed, a disability. But disabilities, whatever form they come in, *need not disqualify.*

Consider, for example, Tom Dempsey who was disabled from birth yet owns one of the most phenomenal NFL records: a 63-yard field goal. I recall watching the game on television in November of 1972. The New Orleans Saints were behind by two points with only one second left on the clock. Tom Dempsey was sent in to try the impossible, which he proved otherwise when he set a record that may never be broken, and in the process won the game for the Saints.

Dealing with the seemingly impossible was nothing new for Tom Dempsey. Born with only half an arm and half a foot on the right side, he never allowed his disability to disqualify him. As a teenager he wanted to play sports. Football was his game. He knew he couldn't play quarterback, running back or lineman, but he believed he could kick field goals with his right foot. So Tom pursued that dream until, with a specially-made shoe and endless hours of practice, he made it a reality. He made the high school team and was recruited to play for a small college. He continued to practice relentlessly and was so consistent in college that he was drafted by the NFL. Most "experts" said "No way!" But *no way* was not in Tom Dempsey's vocabulary.

Monday morning sports pages across the nation heralded the unbelievable feat of Tom's Sunday afternoon heroics. A minister in Minneapolis read it and was overwhelmed. He immediately called the Saint's front office to find out what time they would be practicing. Then he booked a flight to New Orleans and on Tuesday afternoon was standing on the sidelines watching Tom Dempsey kick one field goal after another.

The minister approached Tom and requested fifteen minutes of his time. He asked Tom, "What went through your mind as you stood on the sidelines hoping to get a chance? What did you tell the other ten players in the huddle? And what were your final actions right before your foot came in contact with the ball?"

"First of all, I knew that if the coach called on me I could win the game," replied Tom. "Secondly, I told everyone in the huddle that if they would just block a second longer, I'd get the job done. Thirdly, I measured the exact distance of where I would stand from the holder so that when the ball was snapped there would be no delay."

"And then what did you do?" the minister asked.

"I kicked that ball sixty-three yards and we won the game," Tom said.

"I realize that, but tell me exactly how you felt as you approached the ball and laid your foot into it."

"When I kicked that ball, I put my whole body into it," said Tom.

The minister replied excitedly, "I knew it! That's exactly what Jesus Christ said two thousand years ago!"

"I didn't know they played football back then," quipped Tom.

"They didn't," said the minister, "but Jesus said if any man would lose himself in the serving of others, he would be certain to find life and life abundantly! And young man, if you'll practice that same attitude as you did Sunday afternoon, you will be a success in any endeavor you undertake."

According to all the experts, Tom Dempsey had no business playing in the NFL, much less setting records. But what do the experts know when the right attitude is intact? They can't seem to accept that disabilities need not disqualify.

Chapter 7

Attitude Determines Success—Part One

"Pros are people who do jobs well even when they don't feel like it."

—Will Rogers

It is your Divine destiny to succeed. The Bible says, "Dear friend, I pray above all that you may prosper and be in good health, even as your soul prospers." (3 John 2)

Physical and spiritual prosperity are tied together. The spiritual realm controls success in the natural realm.

The book of Joshua puts it into a formula: "This Book of the Law (the Bible) shall not depart out of your mouth (your speech), but you shall meditate on it day and night (your thoughts), that you may observe to do all that is written within (obedience) and then afterwards"—after you *speak* the Word, after you *think* the Word, after you *obey* the Word— "you shall have good success."

The Creator desires that you be successful in your marriage and in other relationships. You were born to be successful in your health, in your work and in your relationships. There is no force that plots failure—that's left up to the individual.

What Is Success?

You have to define success. If you can't define it, how will you know when you've achieved it? Successful people move progressively and systematically toward goals in life. People without goals do not succeed.

How would you like to watch a football game where there were no goals? A player gets the ball and starts running haphazardly all over the field until he's out of wind. That describes a life that has no goal.

If you're going nowhere, any road will take you there. Ships don't come in; they're brought in. It is necessary for the captain of the ship to have a plan.

Success Is Not Making Lots of Money

If the only reason for living is the accumulation of assets, then life will be very shallow. Money can buy things, but things are not the essence of life.

There are millionaires who have Maalox™ in one hand and crackers in the other, so worried someone is going to get their wealth, they can't even enjoy a meal. I can't guarantee many things, but this I can— someone *is* going to get all of our wealth because all of us are one day going to die and be buried in a suit with the back cut out. I've officiated over 200 funerals and I don't recall one time when the hearse was towing a U-Haul™.

When I first moved to Hooker, Oklahoma, I met one of the local morticians, recently retired. He was rather young to retire from the work he'd done most of his adult life. My obvious question was, "Ray, wasn't your retirement a little premature?"

He replied, "When I started signing all of my letters "eventually yours," I knew it was time to give it up!"

His humorous reply was all too true—life is terminal. None of us are going to get out of this thing called "life" alive. Wealth is not the equivalent of life. Wealth makes a wonderful servant to be used in the right way. But wealth can also be a taskmaster that destroys lives. Attitude makes the difference.

What Is the Practical Definition of Success?

The answer depends upon who you are and what you're all about. To the greedy, rich or poor, success is more, more, more. To the politician, success may mean getting re-elected or attaining more power. To the drug addict, success is the next fix. To many Americans, success is the gratification of the instinctual person—to get what they want, when they want it. But the instinctual person can never be satisfied.

The only One who can satisfy the inner soul is the Creator. I'm often asked, "Gary, what is your definition of success?" Most would assume that success for me would be to be able to walk again. No doubt, that would be nice. That's not my ultimate goal in life, however. Success for me is to be a "wounded healer" to as many hurting people as possible. Whether by writing or speaking or counseling, helping those who are failing to *catch their second wind* is what my life is all about!

Success Is Not Popularity or Acceptance

Success is making a difference in the world in which we live. In doing so, we make some friends and some foes.

Success is to serve your God with all your mind, heart, soul, and body.

Success is serving people—the unlovable as well as the lovable.

Success is giving yourself away to your family, your friends, and even your enemies.

Success is dying to self.

People must have the correct attitude toward success to accomplish their agenda. All success—real and lasting success—comes only as a result of right attitudes. Good attitudes produce good results. Bad attitudes produce bad results, nine times out of eight. It's the universal principle of sowing and reaping. That which we sow we will eventually reap—the bad gets multiplied as well as the good.

Chapter 8

Attitude Determines Success—Part 2

"The Golden Rule is of no use to you whatever unless you realize that it is your move."
                                                    —Dr. Frank Crane

We all aspire to succeed, but so few reach their goals. According to the Social Security Administration, only 2 percent of the American population reach the age of sixty-five financially independent. Twenty-three percent have to work their entire lives. Thirty percent depend on charity. Forty-five percent depend on relatives.

Since it is our true destiny at birth to be successful in all areas of life, why is it that so few of us are? I believe the one determining factor is attitude. Remember attitudes begin in our thought life. You're not *who you think you are,* but rather *you are what you think.* It can be no other way.

In other words, you and I decide. We decide which emotions will rule our lives. We decide whether to accept defeat or climb the unclimbable mountain. We decide to feel inferior or not to feel inferior. The Bible says, "As a man thinks in his heart, so is he." That's a universal principle.

Success is not accidental. Success is not a stroke of luck. It is a by-product of attitude. Attitudes determine success or failure. Your attitude toward people will determine whether you're a friend or a foe. Your spiritual attitude will determine whether there is harmony and peace or discord and chaos in your life. Your attitude toward wealth determines whether or not you'll ever attain it. And if you do, whether it will destroy you or improve your life and the lives of others. Wealth, in and of itself, is neutral.

What Is Attitude?

Webster defines attitude as "a mental position in regard to fact." Has anyone ever told you that you have a bad attitude? Parents, teachers, coaches, and bosses sometimes use the phrase "bad attitude" indiscriminately. It means you're too critical, sarcastic, hard to get along with, or insensitive to the feelings of others. It means you generally disagree just to be disagreeable. In other words, you are a "joyless toad!"

People with bad attitudes whine and pout when they don't get their way about things. They're monsters when people disagree with them. A person with a chronic bad attitude can't keep a wife or a husband, can't keep friends, can't keep a job. We respond much more cheerfully to their departures than to their arrivals. They may have great personalities—but not for humanoids.

What is your attitude? Who is responsible for your attitude, good or bad?

We tend to blame our attitudes on everyone and everything except ourselves. We blame our spouses, the weather, the automobile we're driving. We blame everything from the IRS to PMS. The fact of the matter is, if we could kick the posterior of our most frequent worst enemy, we wouldn't be able to sit for a week!

Our reluctance to take ownership for our misdeeds, as well as our attitudes, has reached the absurd. On June 10, 1987, Paul Harvey's "For What It's Worth Department" reported on this ludicrous litigator in Virginia Beach:

> Eric Edmonds, determined to lose weight, went to Humana Hospital Bayside where surgeons shrank the size of his stomach with the use of staples. Within forty-eight hours Eric suffered a "Big Mac Attack" and sneaked out of his room to raid the hospital refrigerator. He ate so much that he burst his staples. He then filed a $250,000 suit against the hospital for failure to keep its refrigerator locked.

On February 28, 1978:

> Mrs. Gladys Gibbons, of London, brought suit against her professional driving instructor. She told the high court that it was his fault when she hit a tree during her nineteenth driving lesson. Mrs. Gibbons, 55, claimed that Howard Priestly, the instructor, could have prevented the acci-

dent. She testified, "If he had just reached over and hit the brake or switched off the ignition, I might never have hit the tree! But, no . . . all he did was brace himself, close his eyes and shout, 'Now you've bloody done it!'" She charged negligence and wanted Priestly to pay the damages.

Who is responsible for my actions? I am! Who is responsible for my attitude? I am!

David wrote, "This is the day that the Lord has made. I will rejoice in it!" (Psalms 118:24)

That is *choice*; not *chance*. Some people get out of bed in the morning saying, "Good morning, Lord!" while others rise with an entirely different expression in "Good lord, it's morning." We choose our attitudes every morning when we get out of bed. There are those who feel the only way to wake up with a smile on your face is to go to bed at night with a coat hanger in your mouth. That's a bad attitude!

Two men looked out prison bars, one saw mud—the other saw stars. Two men in exactly the same situation but with opposite reactions . . .

A Tennessee newspaper carried the story of two young men who had been jilted in their engagements. Each made a choice about his attitude. One chose to commit suicide by jumping off a bridge. The other chose to write a country-western song that he ultimately sold for $175, 000 in royalties.

You and I choose our attitudes—when life seems great and all is in our favor as well as when circumstances are lousy and seem totally unfair.

A young man attending a prestigious university risked flunking out of medical school as he hovered precariously between a "D" and an "F" in zoology. Family honor, if not ambition, dictated that he make every effort to commit to memory the scientific names of our feathered friends.

Unfortunately, his every effort wasn't enough, even with the aid of memory schemes. He walked into the classroom to take the exam and found ten birds lined up on a single perch. Each bird had a brown sack covering all but its legs. The professor didn't remove the sacks but gave the assignment to identify the birds based on examination of their legs.

The young man sat contemplating for five minutes or so before admitting to himself that he didn't have a prayer. In those five minutes he developed a really bad attitude. In fact, he went ballistic. He stood up at his desk and said, "This is a stupid test, and you are a stupid professor, and this is a stupid university!" He picked up his books, slammed them down on the floor and started to walk out. As he reached the door the professor asked, "Boy, what's your name?" The young man pulled up his pant legs and said, "You guess, Professor, you guess!"

Chapter 9

Attitude Determines Success—Part 3

"*Be willing to have it so. Acceptance of what has happened is the first step in overcoming the consequences of any misfortune.*"

—William James

How Do You Change Your Attitude?

You don't change your attitude with the latest pop psychology—or at least for very long. You change your attitude with good, well-grounded thoughts and ideas. The Bible says, " . . . whatever is true, whatever is noble, whatever is right, whatever is pure, whatever is lovely, whatever is admirable—if anything is excellent or praiseworthy—think about such things." (Philippians 4:8)

> It's immutable. "As a man thinks in his heart, so is he."

It's easy to get mad thinking about things that happened to us in the past. Unresolved anger has proven to be the major cause of clinical depression. It even causes physical disorders. The solution? Let go! Quit concentrating on what has been. A person doesn't exist who hasn't had negative upheavals. The smart ones are those who concentrate on the positive and put energy into the present rather than stoke fires of anger and bitterness from the past. The positive for me is God. He is the healer of broken hearts. He is able to put dreams back together again.

Don't wade in the sewers of yesterday looking for something worth salvaging from your past. Don't look for someone to blame for your failures. In reality, you haven't failed unless you quit trying. You were born to win! Pull yourself up out of the morass and seek the positive with which to surround yourself. You are free to do so no matter what your circumstances—the choice is yours.

Adopt the attitude of the Apostle Paul: "I can do all things through Christ Who gives me strength!"

He penned that while in a diseased, rat-infested jail in Rome. Paul was beaten three times with thirty-nine stripes. (The Romans had flogging down to a science. They knew there was a good chance a person would die of trauma and loss of blood if given forty lashes, so they stopped at thirty-nine. Still, men could, and often did, die from the whip, which was embedded with fragments of bone and metal; it eviscerated them.) Paul was thrown into prison, although he was innocent, on numerous occasions. He was cursed at, spit on, and kicked. He was stoned and left for dead. But he did not whine about suffering for his convictions. He pulled his bleeding body out of the dirt and continued moving forward and upward toward his goal. He was propelled by the right attitude.

Listen to these tremendous words Paul wrote in the midst of an upheaval in his life: "We are hard-pressed on every side, but not crushed; perplexed, but not in despair; persecuted, but not abandoned; struck down, but not destroyed." (2 Corinthians 4:8,9) The Phillips Translation states ". . . we are knocked down, but not knocked out."

Remember, your attitude is not dictated by your circumstances. How *you* dictate your attitude determines your success or your failure. Do you meet obstacles head-on with an attitude of "can do"? Or is your attitude a reactionary one, determined by the obstacles themselves framed by an attitude of "I can't"? The choice is yours. Unless you make a conscious decision, you automatically opt to let circumstances choose for you. Circumstances tend to choose badly.

One afternoon, shortly after my injury, I was in my hospital room having my daily pity party. A good friend of mine rolled into the room and listened to my whining and complaining about all the reasons I had for giving up. He remained silent for awhile and then he said, "Gary let me tell you something. Everyone has been hurt at some point in their lives. There is something all of us could go back and wail about if we chose to. For the sake of your family and your own sake, grow up and get on with your life! Look to the future. Quit worrying about what you've lost and start concentrating on what you've got left. Be thankful God spared your life. And realize tomorrow will be brighter."

Don't people like that wear on your nerves?

Earthquakes and Attitudes

But, he was right. Besides, how could I argue with someone who couldn't move any part of his body below his neck? The only way he was able to operate his electric wheelchair was by the movement of his chin. Talk about receiving an attitude adjustment. It was like he'd worked me over with a crow bar!

Insensitive? Hardly. Sometimes true friendship means tough love. I'd been on my pity pot long enough. It was, just as he said, time to move forward. I had a wife and three children who were depending on me.

Excuses That Kill Attitude

People say, "There's no way I can do that."

"I can't do that" is very close kin to "I don't want to do that." I know, I've been the president of the club! But successful living does not consist of what we *want* to do. Successful living consists of what we *should* do. Attitude is what keeps us on target, or helps us miss the mark.

Here are some common excuses that will capsize attitude:

- "Oh, I'm too old!" Moses was eighty years old when he became the leader of over two million people. Grandma Moses was eighty years old when she started painting, and she sold some of those paintings for thousands of dollars. I can hardly wait until I get to be eighty. I'm going to get a Weed-Eater™, dip it in five gallons of paint, throw it all over a canvas, frame it and sell it!

- "I'm too handicapped!" How handicapped are you? Helen Keller was blind, deaf and mute. She learned to speak without ever having heard a sound and she graduated from college with honors. When I was in grade school, report card day at our house was known as "Helen Keller Day." I'd come home whining and complaining about teachers and subjects and I'd always get the "Helen Keller Speech." I didn't stand a chance.

I'm pro-education, but education *by itself* doesn't determine your success. Attitude does. A man went to a junior high school and applied for a custodial job. When the principal handed him a job application, the applicant said, "I can't read or write."

"Well, you can't work in this school if you can't read or write," said the principal.

So the man went out and started selling cigars door-to-door. He became very good at it and soon rounded up ten of his buddies to help him sell. Eventually he became very wealthy, selling franchises all over America.

A few years later he was invited back to that same junior high school to give a speech on success. After a tremendous lecture, the principal said, "Just imagine what you could have done with an education."

"Yeah, I'd be in this school pushing a broom," replied the millionaire.

Attitude Is Not Determined by Our Circumstances

"If only my circumstances would change, I would change."

Wrong!

However, if we determine to change our attitudes, we'll be equipped to handle whatever circumstances arise. Yes, we're back to making the choice about attitude. We can *get bitter* or we can *get better.* If we choose to be guided by faith and not fear . . . if we'll begin praising and cease pouting . . . if we'll act the victor instead of the victim—then great things will start happening to us. Change your attitude and change your world!

In the counseling I do, I've heard so many men say, "If only my wife was happy, then I'd be happy."

Wrong again!

To be successful you must *act your way to a better way of feeling* instead of *feeling your way to a better way of acting.*

Most of us simply need to make an adjustment in our mind-set concerning who we are. We were created in the very image of our Creator. You are unique— you are truly one of a kind. If you want to succeed, start from where you are right now. Make a difference in *your* world. Bloom where you're planted!

Sabotaging Attitudes

Many people want to succeed but never will because they've sabotaged their attitudes. A person whose thoughts are poisoned by anger and bitterness will never succeed. Many people are filled with regrets and resentments from the past. Many have no defined goals or purpose in life. To some, a six-pack and a 29-inch color TV define success. Past mistakes can sabotage success, if we let them.

You want to succeed—it's inborn in all of us. Change your attitude and become all you were meant to be. Keep the attitudes that are sabotaging you, and you lose. You'll become more disabled than I am. It's impossible to get to the desired destination if you get on the wrong bus. Earl Nightingale was right when he said one form of insanity is to keep doing the same things over and over while expecting different results.

Attitude determines your success. A good attitude results in success. A poor attitude results in failure. The good news? The choice is yours.

Most of the time, changing your attitude *is* catching your *second wind* . . . even in the midst of an upheaval.

Chapter 10

Got Any Jumper Cables?

"Make other people like themselves a little better and you can rest assured they'll like you very much."
—Anthony Robbins

Earthquakes are one of the most devastating of all natural disasters. Some people will never recover from the California earthquake of January 17, 1994. Among those who recover, the experience will deepen their character and help to mold them into champions. One such champion is Emerson Palame.

Emerson, 10, was affected by that early morning quake but he refused to be a victim. As aftershocks became less frequent, Emerson began to play the piano again with one hand. One of his fingers had been crushed by a falling clock as he slept at his grandparents' home.

Emerson knew that doctors would have to amputate a portion of the finger, but he remained confident he'd be able to play the piano with a prosthetic. He wasn't about to let the earthquake keep him from using his natural talent. He also began composing his own music.

"He's a trooper," his father said. "He's being real brave."

Emerson said he tried not to think about his injury. He says, "I'm happy that the earthquakes have stopped and that everything's getting back to normal. I prayed to God and asked Him to help me through this time. And it worked!"

There's nothing much more powerful than an earthquake of great magnitude unless it's the attitude of a ten-year-old champion who refused to be controlled by adverse circumstances. I can assure you, we haven't heard the last of Emerson Palame. If only it were possible to hook up some jumper cables to Emerson's spirit and jump-start about half the people in America.

Earthquakes may not be alterable, but attitudes are, and you and I are in charge of our attitudes. By way of our attitudes, we are in charge of our destinies.

You are in control. It's not your boss, your spouse or the breaks in life that create your attitude. It's you! How you think and how you react to a situation are entirely up to you. The attitude you choose ultimately determines the outcome of your journey. It gets you on the right bus and tells you where to get off.

Let me introduce you to someone who is a living example of the power of attitude. Her name is Phyllis Burdge, and she serves as the editor of my books. Phyllis graduated from college with honors in English. It was apparent from the very beginning that she was gifted in those areas. She taught in a community college shortly after her graduation, but only for a brief while before the multiple sclerosis she'd had for several years began to progressively limit her.

Phyllis experienced neuromuscular difficulties for at least three years before multiple sclerosis (MS) was correctly diagnosed. MS can be a very unforgiving and unpredictable disease of the nervous system. For some people it goes into remission, never to strike again. Others are not as fortunate. For whatever reason, they experience an attack (an exacerbation) every six months or so which slowly drains their bodies of strength and endurance. Their motor skills diminish greatly. Often they progress from an abnormal gait to a cane, then to a walker and eventually to a wheelchair. Problems arise with breathing, talking, and swallowing.

Phyllis did not fall into the first category of people who experience an early remission with minimal progress of the disease. Without warning, she experienced one attack after another. With each one she lost more strength and mobility. She began using a wheelchair just a few short years after the diagnosis was made. At the moment I write this, she is hospitalized in Hays, Kansas, recovering from another attack.

She could have thrown in the towel a long time ago and no one would have blamed her a bit. She lost many things in the process of her illness, but one thing she never lost was her tenacious attitude. Phyllis says she never lost her faith. She doesn't talk about her attitude or her own strength of character. She gives credit to a Higher Power.

"All I have to do is believe," she says. "I have the easy part."

I've never once heard her complain or whine about her condition even though she faces many challenges in her daily life. As a matter of fact, she gives me a "jump start" every time we correspond by letter or telephone. She literally helps me *catch a second wind.*

In 1988, Phyllis received a service dog from Support Dogs, Inc., St. Louis, Missouri. (Dogs are placed at no charge to the recipients or their families and funding comes from grants and donations. You can reach them at: Support Dogs, Inc., 3958 Union Rd., St. Louis, MO 63125, (314) 892-2554.)

Alex was a huge, beautiful golden retriever, trained from a pup to serve his master. Alex opened doors for Phyllis. He pulled her wheelchair up ramps and over long distances. He picked up objects she dropped or things she directed him to such as the telephone, her shoes, a pillow or a hundred other items. (He once picked up a block of postage stamps and gave them to her without damaging a single one.) He helped her up when she fell and supported her physically and emotionally when there was no strength of her own left. If I didn't know better, I would have considered Alex a human—he was more intelligent and compassionate than a lot of people I've run into.

On January 2, 1994, Alex suddenly showed signs of serious illness. He died on January 25. An autopsy revealed cancer of the liver and the spleen. Phyllis was devastated. She had lost more than her best friend; she lost her independence. I called her one evening to express my sorrow and her golden attitude surfaced once again.

"God gave me Alex for five wonderful years," she said. "There will never be another Alex, but He will provide for me once again in a marvelous way."

Amazing!

It was during that conversation I approached her about being my editor. She gladly and graciously accepted with great enthusiasm. I was elated! Anyone with her skills and especially her attitude, I want on my team.

Phyllis is the epitome of what attitude is all about. She focuses on success, not failure; potential, not limitations; strengths, not weaknesses; helpfulness, not helplessness; self fulfillment, not discouragement; positives, not negatives. She focuses on her faith.

It's always been my good fortune to have been influenced by champions of the human race. Phyllis is a champion. In fact, just writing about her has recharged my battery. She is, indeed, a booster cable!

Conclusion

Aftershock

Earthquakes are nothing short of nightmares. The nightmare recurred for Diane Williams and others who had begun to forget the deadly Northridge earthquake when a jarring 5.3-magnitude aftershock shook southern California once again. (Aftershock? Sounds like an earthquake to me.)

"I had just finally started to calm down," said Williams, 42, of Van Nuys. "This one really shook me up."

That's the way the upheavals of life are, too. About the time we think we're moving on with life—bam!—an aftershock hits us.

- For the widow, it's the photograph she finds in a cluttered drawer that brings back so many memories and so many tears.

- For the divorcee, it's the letter that was written years ago and speaks of love that will never die.

- For the mother, it's the photograph of a son who went "haywire" on drugs and now serves a prison term.

This list of "aftershocks" could go on and on.

For me, it was the trip to the track field last week. I watched my son run as I used to and I longed so much to run again with him.

Aftershocks jar us into the cold reality that what has happened is real; the earthquake was a nightmare come true. That's why attitudes are so very important. They not only help us withstand the upheavals of life, they brace us for the aftershocks certain to follow. As I write the final pages of *Earthquakes and Attitudes*, I want to share with you some nuts and bolts that will hopefully give all this some tangibility and make it practical:

- The attitude process is simple and three-fold—purpose, commitment, repetition.

- Keep in mind that developing or changing an attitude takes time. It usually doesn't happen overnight. Don't expect it to be an easy task, but expect it to be a worthwhile one.

- Try to have a positive influence on others. Attitudes are like boomerangs . . . what goes around comes around. This means, of course, that some days you will have to *act* better than you *feel*.

- Associate with positive, solution-oriented people. Spend time with people who "pick you up," who encourage you to do better and be better. Take advantage of their energy and enthusiasm. Literally, feed off of their attitudes. Everybody needs a cheerleader for reinforcement and support—find yours.

- Don't hold a grudge. Resentments of any kind amount to negative feelings that absolutely have no productive gain. Lose them! Audit your books and cancel all debts you've recorded.

- Read good books. Listen to good music. Turn off the electronic sewer pipe (TV) and listen to some motivational speeches or tapes of faith-building sermons. Don't reject this paragraph until you've *tried* it!

- Pronounce procrastination a thing of the past. Begin *today* to set goals that will propel you onward and upward in pursuit of them.

- Rely upon the grace of God. He told the apostle Paul, who experienced many upheavals, "My grace is sufficient for you." Grace is the strength—the power—we need, *when* we need it!

At times I'm tempted to write something like, "May you be spared any major problems." However, that is unrealistic as well as counterproductive in its intent, for, "Our afflictions bring about perseverance, and perseverance, character, and character, hope, and hope will not disappoint for Love has been poured into our hearts by the Holy Spirit." (Romans 5:3-5)

And that is truly *catching your second wind!*

Give the Gift
of Inspiration and Hope
to Your Loved Ones
and Friends

ORDER FORM

YES, I want _____ copies of *Earthquakes and Attitudes: Turn Your Obstacles Into Opportunities* at $14.95 each, plus $3 shipping per book (Colorado residents please add $.90 state sales tax per book). Canadian orders must be accompanied by a postal money order in U.S. funds. Allow 15 days for delivery.

☐ **YES**, I am interested in having Gary Moore speak or give a seminar on "Catch Your Second Wind" to my company, association, school, or organization. Please send information.

My check or money order for $_____ is enclosed.
Please charge my ☐ Visa ☐ MasterCard

Name _____ Phone _____

Organization _____

Address _____

City/State/Zip _____

Card # _____ Exp. Date _____

Signature _____

Please make your check payable and return to:

Carpe Diem! Publishers
P.O. Box 1994
Loveland, CO 80539

Or call your credit card order to:
1-800-821-5260